# Life Lines

## A patient's perspective on life with Parkinson's Disease and Cancer

## by Anthony Edey

### with illustrations by Iris Edey

# *Life Lines*

Iris Enterprises

Cover art and Illustrations by Iris Edey
Cover and text design by Susan Picatti

04  03  02  01  00          5  4  3  2  1

ISBN:1-58619-012-1
Library of Congress Catalog Card Number: 00-100509

First Printing February 2000
Printed in the United States

ELTON-WOLF PUBLISHING

Published by Elton Wolf Publishing
Seattle, Washington

2505 - 2nd Avenue, Ste. 515 • Seattle, Washington 98121
e-mail:info@elton-wolf.com • Internet: www.elton-wolf.com
Seattle • Vancouver • Los Angeles • Milwaukee • Denver • Portland

## Dedication

*For my wife,*
*without whose love and care none of these lines would*
*have been possible. My feelings for her*
*were captured in this 39th anniversary poem:*

*If it should be*

*that she can love*

*one such as me,*

*then, Lord above,*

*I would defer*

*all Heaven's bliss*

*to spend with her*

*more days like this.*

*Drawings of flowers will be found throughout this book,*
*symbolizing the natural beauty and goodness which form a backdrop*
*to the story. It is fitting that the first drawing should be of an iris: not*
*only is that the name of the artist, it is also a flower which is*
*traditionally known as 'the messenger.'*

# *Foreword*

I was immensely pleased to be offered the opportunity of introducing this book by my patient, Tony Edey, of reflections on his encounters with two gritty diseases and the medical establishment. I live in "the house set on a hill" mentioned in the first piece and it fell to me to break the news to him that he has Parkinson's disease. I have seen him regularly in the course of helping him to manage that disease through the following years and can testify that he is meeting those challenges head on and with aplomb, grace and wit, all attributes which come through loud and clear in these pieces.

This book gives us a glimpse into the heart of a man who was able to enter that long, dark and unknown medical tunnel only to emerge at the other end still laughing and with a wink at the human condition. It is a very long time since I have laughed out loud while reading a poem as I did repeatedly while reading this work.

I am confident that you will find this book as enjoyable and genuinely therapeutic as I did.

*Jack M Hutton MD*
*Port Townsend WA.*

# *Contents*

# *Preface*

Not long ago I was a busy mining engineer, traveling the world with my artist wife, skilled in planning flight connections and in finding my way around airports and hotels in foreign lands. There seemed to be no reason why this charmed existence should not continue until I reached a normal retirement age in six or seven years. All of this changed in a moment, though, when I was diagnosed as having Parkinson's disease. The promise of steady physical deterioration which is inherent in this disease, was in stark contrast to my good health at the time. This shock, coupled with a natural reluctance to take life's twists too seriously, led to the starting of the first group of poems, presented in this book under the title *"Shaking With Laughter."*

The next year brought another medical surprise in the form of an itchy nose which, on investigation, proved to be a well-developed melanoma. Four operations were required over the following weeks to find and remove the tumor and patch the resulting hole: this then led to a series of radiation treatments and to two further surgical repair procedures which fol-

lowed later. These experiences triggered the second series of verses included here under the title *"An Interesting Case."*

The last group of poems in this collection, titled *"Afterthoughts"*, express my feelings of relief and gratitude as the remission of the cancer lengthened past the most dangerous period and the Parkinson's disease proved manageable, at least for the time being.

Most of these poems were written, or at least started, during the time when the events concerned were actually happening. Others were based on notes or couplets which were discovered later on odd scraps of paper. Some were complete in 30 minutes; others took six weeks or more.

I am convinced that two major reasons for my current good health were the strong family support I enjoyed and the natural beauty with which my home is both filled and surrounded. Those themes are reflected here in the cover art and illustrative drawings by my artist wife, Iris, whose skill in the garden is matched by her talent with pen, palette and brush.

The Anemone makes a suitable introduction to this section.
Known as the 'windflower', it does a good job of keeping its upright
poise even when shaken by the wind. Its folk-lore symbolism of
'expectations' relates well to a disease where, although there
are many downside expectations, the
current reality remains very beautiful.

# Part 1:

# *Shaking With Laughter*

*reflections in rhyme*

*on*

*Parkinson's disease*

*Learning that one has a disease such as Parkinson's cannot be described as a happy event without risking the writer's credibility. The way in which this news came to us, though, was surprisingly tranquil and warm and many of its aspects have since grown on us as having been special and touching. In fact, it turned out to be the first of many occasions on which our dominant impressions, both at the time and in retrospect, were to be of the immense humanity and compassion of the medical professions, a conclusion not at all in line with the prevailing wisdom.*

# *Diagnosis*

We sought an explanation, though without too much alarm,
About my problem swinging a recalcitrant left arm.
It worked well when I gave it simple duties to perform
Like playing on a keyboard or just typing up a storm.

But walking's automatic, it's just done without a thought,
Right foot, left arm together, each one swinging when it ought.
This system wasn't working, though, the arm just hung there limp,
The hand clenched over-tightly and the posture like a chimp.

We really thought I'd scarred my brain when knocked out by a fall,
The impact knocked me silly but there'd seemed no harm at all.
Perhaps somewhere inside, though, there were scars or bleeding still.
They could provide the reasons for my arm's lack of free will.

I'd also had Bell's Palsy, twice in fact, once on each side,
The second time quite badly, which had left us petrified.
That nasty little number paralyzes half your face
But, thanks to massive steroids, it had vanished without trace.

It seemed some part of Bell's had stayed and maybe could have spread
To cut communication links between my arms and head.
The doctor viewed the CAT scans, poked and prodded with great care,
"You're off to the neurologist, I think there's something there."

The site of this appointment was a house up on a hill,
Of true Victorian grace and style and cared for with great skill.
The garden told a story, too, of loving work and care,
Such auras can't be purchased – real people must be there.

Inside was clearly lived in, warm and cluttered as a home,
All wood and books and leather, not a single piece of chrome.
This was no sterile office, no museum of drug and knife,
This was a house for people who were celebrating life.

The questions were quite simple, observations, tests galore,
Each limb and joint examined, searching for a fatal flaw.
It all seemed very normal, nothing wrong except the arm.
The tone of all the questions gave no cause for real alarm.

The answer then came quickly, given simply, face to face,
There was no ancient lesion, Bell's had passed without a trace.
The simple diagnosis was one certain not to please,
I had begun the journey known as Parkinson's Disease.

*Pansy,*
*symbolizing thoughtfulness*

*This poem remembers wise advice given by a friend: "tell people so they can show you that they care." She was absolutely right and we have been continually comforted, humbled and blessed by the knowledge that so many people do in fact care, want to care and are usually grateful for an opportunity to care.*

# *Shakin' and Stirred*

When first you have the knowledge of a medical condition
It's natural to view it as a personal affair.
Eventually the family must know the situation
But generally it's not the sort of gossip that you share.

How wrong! I soon received a firm but gentle admonition,
Sent by a gallant lady newly freed from cancer's snare.
She said "Tell one and all – for this will drive out inhibition
And let so many people drop their masks and show they care."

My friend was quite correct in sending me that bold prediction,
In urging me to trust the human spirit's giving ways.
There must have been a thousand ways I gained from this affliction,
A surplus I could store to tide me over leaner days.

It's true – this generosity is simple fact not fiction,
My heart's been warmed so often by some caring deed or word.
Unlike James Bond's martini I have this great benediction –
Not only am I shakin' but my spirit's often stirred.

*Parkinson's disease is caused by deterioration in the function of a small gland situated in the back of the head, called the* substantia nigra. *This guilty gland made a convenient target for the anger and fear which undoubtedly existed beneath my apparently philosophical acceptance of the diagnosis. A succession of rather bitter little verses emerged within a few days, giving vent to feelings which have had no other expression or, so far as I know, any existence.*

# *The Guilty Gland*

### I

*Substantia Nigra* is its name,
Smooth muscle function is its game.
Sadly if it doesn't work –
Stiffness, slowness, shake and jerk.

### II

My wretched *substantia nigra*
Is clearly not up to its job.
And since it won't show much improvement
I'll probably end up a slob.

### III

We're all blessed with *substantia nigras*,
They're walnut-sized lumps in the brain.
In Parkinson's they're what's not working,
With results that are, simply, a pain.

### IV

*Substantia Nigra* is my name,
Making dopa is my game.
If by chance my job I shirk,
Lots of you ain't gonna work.

### V

*Substantia Nigra* means things look
Significantly black.
In fact, if I could find a spare,
I'd send my old one back!

*The thoughts that were induced by my growing awareness of future physical deterioration ranged from the whimsical and comic to the sad and more than a little self-pitying. These two poems reflect the lighter end of that range.*

# *Symptoms*

It seems that my shoulder
Is fast getting older.
It moves pretty well but it creaks.

Moreover my knees
Are not bending with ease.
They crackle and pop, and one squeaks.

My stiffened left ankle
Is starting to rankle.
It hasn't moved freely for weeks.

Discussion of plumbing
Is quite unbecoming.
You simply don't talk about leaks!

The lesson I gather
From all of this blather
Has value for all of us freaks,

Leave crying for after:
There's still room for laughter.
Who cares if we're shaky antiques?

# *Slow Hands*

The pop song claimed, some  years ago,
That girls like men whose hands are slow.
Prefer them with an easy touch,
Their other traits don't count for much.


I, then, must drive them half-way mad,
My left hand works so slow it's sad.
The right one, though, works good as new:
Its easy touch will do for two.


At last I think I understand
Why girls are putty in my hand.
The problem with this stratagem?
Remembering what to do with 'em!

*Sweet pea, traditionally*
*associated with 'delicate pleasure.'*

*Although I was never a particularly good performer on piano or organ, those instruments had played an important part in my life and the dream was always there of some day doing some serious practice and seeing how good I could be. My attempts to play again under these new circumstances, though, brought occasional satisfaction but a lot of frustration, as reflected in the next poems. The disease steadily eroded even that minimal level of satisfaction, however, until it became impossible to pretend any longer that I was going to be the next Horowitz and I accepted the (apparent) end of that feature of my life.*

# *The Piano*

How then to view the piano?  Test supreme,
Whose judgment penetrates the hands' deceit.
My playing, always fractured, still can seem
For fleeting, precious seconds, true and sweet.
The left hand falters, though, as in a dream
And promptly turns my Mozart to defeat.


Those lower chords are tardy, often bland.
The touch is clumsy, scales and trills are gone.
Yet, so it seems to me, my other hand
Has taken on new strength and grace of tone.
So nature compensates, we understand,
And no half man is forced to play alone.

*Anthony Edey*

# The Piano — Sequel

For most of us stumbling occasional pianists,
Playing's a personal confidence trick.
We hit lots of notes, even some from the music.
Play fast bits too slowly and *lento's* too quick.

But none of this matters, as long as we're able
To feel in our souls that our fumbling hands
Still manage to make, for a phrase or a passage,
Exactly the music our heart understands.

A tiny achievement, but that much is vital
For playing without it is just making noise.
Without the illusion of making true music
The lid should be closed. Go and find other toys.

I'll close then the piano, with thanks for the pleasure
That playing has given me over the years.
Just sometimes I met there the greats of the keyboard
And echoed their playing, at least to my ears.

That's more than sufficient for one mortal lifetime.
Those transient perfections were gold-dust to me.
They're all in the past, though. A new era beckons:
Henceforth I will play *all* the notes (on CD).

# *The Piano — Again*

Time to stop these vain pretensions,
There's no music here at all.
I was bad enough two-handed,
One hand drives me up the wall.

Lefty is completely frozen
Hardly even tries to play.
No dexterity or timing,
Can't distinguish C from A.

If I concentrate completely
Lefty can improve somewhat.
But the price I pay is dreadful
'Cuz the right hand goes to pot!

While my brain is focused leftwards
Chaos strikes the other side.
Briefly left without direction
Poor old Righty's mystified.

Sadly it's no longer worth it,
Parkinson's has spread its curse.
There's no chance of real music,
And it's quickly getting worse.

Making music's been a blessing,
Minor talent, major fun.
Some regrets I wasn't better,
(All those practices un-done).

Still, despite my talent's limits
Some notes landed where they should.
This my musical memorial,
"Now and then a phrase was good."

*Dog rose, the traditional meaning*
*of pleasure with pain describes my playing very well:*
*I had most of the pleasure.*

*Within a year or so of diagnosis, Parkinson's disease became incompatible with some aspects of a mining engineer's life. Most obviously, it introduced an unacceptable level of risk into visits to underground mines: more subtly, it made intensive travel intolerable as increased fatigue and the difficulty of spending long periods in confined spaces took their toll. For a time, these problems were adequately compensated for by traveling First Class and better still, by traveling with my wife. Even these comforts were often unavailable or inadequate, though, and the experience became progressively more frustrating and uncomfortable. These verses were written in an airport lounge while trying to connect between Elko, Nevada and Port Angeles, Washington.*

# Reflections on a Flight

Just recently, it came to pass
I learned a lesson about class
By sitting in Row 22,
Not up front with the chosen few.

The flight was short enough, I thought,
Economy was what I bought.
I could survive that little while
As long as I sat on the aisle.

But headwinds brought a different fate,
I reached the gate some minutes late.
No precious aisle, no 14D,
Row 22, seats B or E.

I fought my way back down the plane,
Quite tempted to get off again.
Each look seemed to excoriate
This thoughtless man who'd made them late.

And next to every vacant place,
A look of hope. Then every face
Changed to alarm as I drew near,
"He can't be going to sit down here!"

But soon I'm there, a cosy fit
Inside the space where I must sit.
My carry-on's beneath the seat
But where to put my aching feet?

My arm by now is full of pain,
The tremor's started up again.
It really needs a thorough stretch,
But what a welcome that would fetch!

My neighbor's made it clear to all
She didn't want me there at all.
Her posture firmly now avers
The armrest is, quite simply, hers.

I pull the arm to still the quiver,
Lest it should shake the lady's liver.
I stretch a leg to ease the pain
But find her knee's there first again.

It even feels quite hard to breathe
Without impinging on her sleeve.
As all my limits thus I probe,
I fast become a claustrophobe.

Refreshments bring a test of will,
Just go without or risk a spill?
One careless twitch could cause a splash
As ginger ale and elbows clash.

Peanuts and pretzels, such a meal
Hardly distracts from what you feel.
Old habits win, though: seems that we
Cannot reject what's offered free.

What then the message? Where's the beef
In all this fleeting, flying grief?
If with the shakes you're really cursed,
Don't save the pennies, TRAVEL FIRST!

Or, if you find that price too high
For those few minutes in the sky,
Read carefully this silly poem,
Then call it off and STAY AT HOME!

*Very occasionally circumstances con-spire to create a situation which gives some perspective to our often confused existence. One such 'revelation' came to me in Calgary airport while in transit between ill-matched flights on a holiday weekend. The terminal was deserted and sterile and I was in the middle of a complex itinerary, going to a place I really did not want to go. These lines appeared in minutes as I tried to sort out in my mind what I was doing with my life. It would be nice to record that all of this insight brought about an instant change in lifestyle: such a change did indeed happen a short time later but it was induced by cancer rather than wisdom.*

# *Why Work?*

Why do I work?  Why am I on this plane?
What has me flying to some mine again,
Leaving behind my wife, so much held dear?
What can be strong enough to draw me here?

Perhaps it's money, seizing one last fee,
Adding to savings, more security
For riding out those storms of life and health
Which so destroy the living, steal their wealth.

Maybe it's just a hunt for self respect
A clinging to the world of the select,
Of ounces, dollars, tonnes and courier packs
Where even last week's news must go by fax.

Then there's the fact that I just love to be
With miners, my preferred fraternity.
Testing my wits, my skills, my working worth,
Wresting obedience from the solid earth.

If truth be told, maybe I fear to try
To cope with life without identity.
Could I be active, satisfied, fulfilled
With pen and piano (things that can't be billed).

And then there's Parkinson, my shaky friend,
Who's also working to ensure an end
To all this life of travel, mines and fun;
Stealing my final years so dearly won.

He's stiffened my joints, toyed with my balance too,
Made climbing ladders not a thing to do.
The mind's OK, though, now and then inspired.
It all just leaves me so profoundly tired.

This way is mad, no future should consist
Of mines and airports, deadlines made or missed.
Who in his mind would choose this frenzied way
When close at hand there waits a gentler day?

There is no need to fear the life that waits
Beyond the first small death, retirement's gates.
My future is pre-blessed, tho' short or long,
With family and friends I can't go wrong.

*Wallflower, representing*
*faithfulness in adversity*

*Interwoven with the moments of humor are the inevitable times when something reminds us of the less palatable aspects of Parkinson's. One such reminder for me was the sight of the irrepressible grin on the face of a small grandson. Being blessed with many memories of happy hugs from that same little comic, as well as of the brevity of two year old memories, it was suddenly very important to know how he will remember his Grandpa.*

# *Sam*

I wonder how Sam will remember his Grandpa.
I wonder what image I'll leave on his mind.
Will there be echoes of warmth and of laughter?
Will there be memories of strength left behind?
Or only dim shadows of shaky caresses,
Embarrassing moments, with love intertwined.


I need Sam to grow, to mature while I'm healthy
And able to play and to take him for walks:
To share in some music, some long bedtime stories,
Some jokes and some mischief, a few manly talks.
Such things would implant a true picture of Grandpa,
Too real to be drowned by the illness that stalks.


Small children are programmed to learn for the future,
Absorbing the present, rejecting the past.
Their strongest emotions are prone to displacement
And even their fondest recalls may fade fast.
Too soon they grow older and memory lengthens
And few early things are embedded to last.

If Sam cannot hasten to that stage of knowing,
Nor quicken his growth to an age to retain
Good lasting impressions to represent Grandpa,
A profile that I can be sure he'll retain,
I'll just have to wait then, unshaken, unbending,
Refusing to yield to this flaw in my brain


These clear normal images must be burned deeply,
Too strongly, too cleanly to blur in a while.
Whatever temptations may come to beguile me
I'll not yield an inch, lest it grow to a mile.
I will be remembered as strong, normal Grandpa.
I will leave an image that launches Sam's smile.

*Sam, age two, about the time this poem
was written.*

*This next poem is an awkward commentary on an awkward aspect of the disease — the patient's nuisance value to himself and those around him, and the problem of coping gently with well-intentioned but misguided help.*

# *Word Play**

If blessed with full dexterity
You surely feel that you're all right.
The opposite is sinister, you just get left
Behind when folding sheets.

The deft
Are over-kind, giving help
When all you need is extra time:
Maybe a lot of it.

Time to sort out money for the cashier.
Time to get the change back in a pocket.
Time to tie laces, button shirts, dry dishes, eat spaghetti.

Time to do it irritatingly slowly,
Maddeningly clumsily,
But by yourself.

How sad that the price of independence
Is being an interference.

Now *that* is sinister all right!

• Latin: dexter = right;   sinister = left

*Fashions in good health come and go like the weather, but smoking has been on the 'bad' list for many years. It was therefore a surprise to read that it is possible that the chemical whose presence is believed to cause the pleasure from smoking is the very substance whose lack causes Parkinson's disease.*

# *The Final Cure*

I hear that I ought to start smoking,
Just try a medicinal pack.
Inhale all the nice levadopa
My little gray cells seem to lack.

I hear that the feeling-good factor
Is just what I'm missing of late.
A packet of Gaulloise should fix it,
I'd happily asphyxiate.

It's really a strange contradiction
That smoking could see this thing off.
Instead of a long life of shaking
I'd die nice and slow of a cough!

On balance it seems quite apparent,
The treatment is worse than the cure.
Though Parkinson's may not be perfect,
It's better than smoking, for sure.

*In 1996, the whole television-watching world was touched and saddened by the spectacle of Muhammad Ali lighting the Olympic flame in Atlanta and of his struggle to control his tremor. Later on during the Games, many were also amazed and touched to see news clips of Ali meeting the athletes and public and to notice that he still displayed the spirit and good humor that were his trademarks in his fighting days. Clearly, he is as little afraid of this latest opponent as he was of Foreman or Frazier in those earlier battles. In this, too, he is The Greatest.*

# The Lighting of the Flame

This Parkinson's business is really a curse.
It's not too bad now but will surely get worse.
You know it won't stop 'til you're safe in the hearse
And sometimes it carries you down.

I see what it's done to Muhammad Ali,
And can't help but think that will happen to me.
It's really not very encouraging, see?
But don't let it carry you down.

Ali was a boxer, the world's Number One.
He stung and he floated, had plenty of fun.
Danced round his opponents, just waiting to stun,
And nothing could carry him down.

Now Parkinson has him, he's slow and he shakes,
Must carefully plan every step that he takes.
Each day is a battle from when he awakes,
Still, nothing has carried him down.

The lesson to learn if you're some way bereft,
Whenever you feel less than perfectly deft:
It's not what you've lost – it's the things you have left
That won't let life carry you down.

'It's not over 'til it's over' is as true with Parkinson's disease as any other aspect of life. Steady deterioration had become an established aspect of my life when a visit to the neurologist yielded a prescription for a different medication. This one was a dopamine agonist, a substance which fools the brain cells into thinking that it is the missing dopamine. The results clearly exceeded my expectations.

# *Permax*™

I got rather used to deterioration
As being the natural Parkinson's way.
I knew that the future held more degradation
But focused on getting the best from each day.
I even found comfort in grasping that future,
In staying the course as I slid down the hill.
But that sort of thinking was thrown to confusion
By Permax, the name of a little pink pill.

It gave the receptors on some of my brain cells
A good dose of something they clearly had lacked.
Whatever the reasons, the change was amazing,
This Permax worked wonders, and that was a fact.
An instant improvement hit all of my symptoms,
My limbs all felt free and the tremor was still.
It's not very often you get to start over,
And all for the price of a little pink pill.

The ultimate test had to be the piano
Where, all unexpected, a bass note appeared.
Not only on time but the right one, amazing,
The first time that miracle's happened in years.
So now it's the keyboard for practice in earnest,
Take up this new chance to see how I can play.
There's no way to know how long Permax will manage
To take the disease and just hide it away.

# *Life on the Pill*

One thing that you know if you've Parkinson's curse,
Your basic disease just goes on getting worse.
For all the research and announcements of cures,
Though pills help the symptoms, the problem endures.

But symptoms are just what you're fighting each day,
So why not wish all of your problems away?
Since any relief represents quite a thrill,
Try Permax, the little pink Parkinson's pill.

What happens when all of your left side's a-shake,
Or turning in bed makes the whole house awake?
When nothing, it seems, can stay static or still,
Take Permax,  the little pink Parkinson's pill.

When limbs are a-quiver and joints become stiff,
When taking a stroll feels like climbing a cliff;
When all of your muscles feel ancient and ill,
Take Permax, the little pink Parkinson's pill.

Your smile is lop-sided? No trouble at all.
You're losing your balance and tending to fall?
No bass in your music? You're in for a thrill
With Permax, the little pink Parkinson's pill.

This list could go on 'til I run out of rhymes
Extolling the joys of these wonderful times.
So if the pill's name is eluding you still,
It's Permax, the little pink Parkinson's pill.

*Not long after completing the previous verses on the joys of Permax, that particular drug was 'fired' in favor of a competitor which is supposed to do essentially the same thing for a fraction of the cost. As the next poems show, the transition was not easy and the eventual result is less than perfect. All in all, though, it is very effective and we are grateful for that.*

# *A Change of Agonist*

Those little pink pills
Surely helped with my ills
They worked very well in their turn.
However, the price
Was not very nice
They think we have money to burn!

So our Doctor Hutton,
Who doesn't miss nuttin',
Decided a change should take place.
Since Requip would be
A lot cheaper for me,
Poor Permax was out in disgrace.

The first Requip dose
Was not even close
With nausea my biggest complaint.
I'd start feeling ill
Right after each pill
And also I'd often feel faint.

These side-effects stayed
For weeks as we made
Adjustments to timing and diet.
Before, with or later
Than meat and potato
Each way we could think of we'd try it.

It's all settled now,
Though I just don't know how,
It has to suffice that I say
That gloomy old verse,
As my left hand got worse,
Does not tell the truth of today.

What's happened is mad:
Though my side's pretty bad,
And often seems stuck in Dead Slow,
The Requip's arranged
That most everything's changed
I'm playing p-i-a-n-o!

# PD's Minefield

There's no doubt, PD's a nuisance,
Blunts one's physical prowess.
But for some its harshest impact
Is its power to create stress.

If you've never had the pleasure
Of an ailment like PD,
It's not easy to imagine
How pervasive stress can be.

For example, take a dinner
Hosted by some lifelong friends.
Just a perfect relaxation?
Yes, perhaps; it all depends.

As you come in to the table,
Appetites and thirsts are keen.
All is rapt anticipation
So enticing is the scene.

Splendid cloth of Irish linen,
Diamond brightness in the glass;
Silver gleams around the table,
Fragrant dishes wait to pass.

And, the final tempting touches,
Long stemmed glasses, Cabernet.
But your seasoned PD patient
Sees it all another way.

Reaching out for salt or pepper,
Not as easy as it sounds.
Handing jugs of sauce or gravy,
Chances for a spill abound.

PD has to plan with caution
Every movement that  he makes.
Not for him the casual gesture;
His fortes are jerks and shakes.

Through his eyes the festive table
Looks more like a field of mines.
Judging from his past experience,
Cabernets are stains, not wines.

*The petunia, bearing the*
*message to 'never despair"*

*The cactus has much in common with cancer.*
*Its sharp spines can inflict much pain but it is*
*also capable of displaying a beauty which can*
*make the spines seem almost irrelevant.*

# Part 2:

# *An Interesting Case*

## *Melanoma without melancholy*

*The skirmish with skin cancer which led to this set of poems came right out of the blue. One minute we were trying to find a solution to what seemed to be nothing more than a persistent itch on my nose and the next we were meeting experts on radiation therapy and chemotherapy. Add on the news that my chance of living for five years free of cancer was about one in three, and I felt that I had discovered a thrill equivalent to bungee-jumping. The first of these poems was written in gratitude to Dr Paul Thompson, the dermatological sleuth who first tracked down the elusive tumor. He can still hardly believe it himself, so slender was the evidence.*

# *Diagnosis*

The ancient men of wisdom told it so,
That mighty oaks from little acorns grow.
A less romantic modern twist on which
Has melanoma starting with an itch!

My nose had shown a spot some years ago:
'Sun-damaged skin' the worst the lab could show.
A minor sore would come and disappear
But, all in all, the nose looked crystal clear...

But for the itch: the only sign I had,
A pesky, teeny itch that drove me mad.
Nothing to see, no brown or angry patch.
One itch alone, just begging me to scratch.

Nothing could stop it, pressure, cold or heat.
No salve could save me from its tickly beat.
Finally, its nuisance value to confirm,
Me and my nose went off to see the 'derm'.

His practiced eye saw nothing to alarm
But, to be safe, some tests would do no harm.
Even the lab near missed the sign that tells
Of desmoplastic melanoma's cells.

At once the war began, the vital race
To clear this fell intruder from my face.
Six operations, radiation's worst,
All for an itch, for so it seemed at first.

So if your hair is red, complexion pale
Just think again the oak and acorn tale.
That sore or spot (or itch) on nose or chin,
Go have it checked, it just could save your skin!

# *My Special Nose*

It's really not difficult, having a nose.
Just about everyone's got one of those.
We couldn't start life without one if we chose.
So what is so special 'bout mine?

Why would those legions of medical chaps
Plaster their walls with my best nasal snaps?
Could it just be that, maybe and perhaps,
There *is* something special 'bout mine?

Last year if you'd studied my profile so pure,
Although you'd have found it a joy, to be sure,
Apart from its beauty and general allure
You'd see nothing special 'bout mine.

And that's just the point that I'm trying to make,
The reason for all of those photos they take,
A dormant volcano just waiting to wake,
*That's* what was so special 'bout mine.

A vast melanoma was cooking inside,
It went pretty deep and was certainly wide.
You wonder how such a big tumor could hide
Inside a proboscis like mine!

No give-away margins, no pigment at all,
Not one of the clues in the chart on the wall.
To biopsy that was a difficult call
On such slender symptoms as mine.

One glance at the lab work and doubt was all gone,
Six trips to the surgeon before it was done,
Two grafts, some electrons to round out the fun
They had with that special of mine.

And but for that itch I would never have thought
That seeing a 'derm' was a thing that I ought.
But just at the critical time it was caught,
That quite special tumor of mine.

So this is the lesson to learn from my nose;
When watching a lesion to see how it grows,
It's risky to wait 'til it obviously shows,
You might have a special like mine!

*Rosa rugosa,*
*thorny but exquisite*

*The next two poems represent front-line reaction at its most direct. They were written in hospital waiting rooms and were obviously a part of my defense mechanism. I suppose that as long as you are busy making fun of your own reactions, you have less time to pay attention to what is happening to you, let alone to think thoughts about the suddenly uncertain future. Whatever the reasons, though, there were very few parts of this whole performance which we found to be totally devoid of comic aspects.*

# *Tumor I*

The first step was test excavation
To see if the growth was confined
To only the shallowest tissues;
Then fate would have truly been kind.

Away to the lab went the samples
For slicing and staining, to show
Through full microscopic appraisal
If all of it's out the first go.

The truth was, you had quite a whopper,
A growth that was both deep and wide.
A challenge for all of those experts
To find where it's trying to hide.

They poked and they pried and took pictures
By X-ray and then MRI.
Reviewed with great care all the options
To see what's the next thing to try.

At last the best course was decided
They'd try excavation again.
Take more of the nose and surroundings,
But try to stay clear of the brain.

What's left will be somewhat unbalanced
A rather astonishing sight.
At least it'll help to distinguish
Which side has been left and which right.

The left's quite all right – it's still present,
Just more or less left as before.
The right is not right, though, some's missing
And what's left just feels downright sore.

# *Tumor II*

There's nothing quite like your own tumor
To turn the whole cancer thing real.
To strip off the cover of humor
And make you aware what you feel.

You're told you've a rare melanoma,
That sets you apart from the crowd.
You've just scored a medical homer!
You feel strangely special and proud.

It's not really something to wish for,
A time-bomb that ticks in your face.
How lucky there's this consolation,
At least you're an interesting case.

*The entire surgical system seems intended to ensure that the patient remembers little about the experience. It is even more certain that one is left in no condition or mood for solving poetic problems of meter and rhyming plan. That is my only excuse for the fact that the pieces included next are disjointed, staccato and brief.*

# *Surgery – Before*

Nurses dressed in floral coats,
Doctors bustling by in white.

None of this seems too severe,
Nothing yet to cause a fright.

This is just the opening act,
Vital, though, their busy tasks.

Heavy hitters come on next
Blue pajamas, hats and masks.

No more people, merely shapes,
Busy voices, caring eyes.

Tea-tray lights, then all this fades...

# *Surgery – After*

Flowers on the ceiling - last time there were birds.
Something to look at, calm the jumpy nerves.

Busy feet, blue shapes rush by.
Either an emergency or lunch.

But I am quite alone.
Everyone is so busy.
Maybe they've forgotten me …

Shower cap, blue gown,
Mask and pretty eyes, kind eyes …
soft voice saying my name …
it must be over ….

Awake this time, IV hurts.
There's something wrong with my face.
Cheerful, fat porter, dressed like a doctor,
Big doors, people upside-down.

There is my wife, healing with a smile,
And, joy of joys, my daughter,
Straight from the airport, straight from London.

Now I can let go.
All is well.

# *IF*

(with apologies to Rudyard Kipling)

IF you can keep your face when all around you
Are all dressed up in masks and pale blue smocks,

IF you can keep your nerve when all you're wearing
Is half a dress and funny little socks,

IF you can contemplate without a tremor
Them cutting off your nose to save your life,

IF you can close your eyes and just breathe deeply

All will be well, my son.

*More nonsense rhymes, born of either a keen sense of the ridiculous or pure terror. Somehow it was important to lampoon the legions in white coats (or trendy blue surgical scrubs), toting the all-important stethoscopes, who have so much power over you at such times.*

# *Gut Humor*

Of all the strange sayings in English
Here's one that is certainly daft.
A phrase that we use rather often,
Describing how hard we have laughed.

We say that he "had us in stitches"
A truly hilarious feel.
It's not quite so funny for some, though,
When stitches are in you for real.

On waking from facial excisions
And grafting of skin to the wound,
I found my nose tied on with stitches,
Big black ones like in a cartoon.

The surgeon had clearly been jesting,
Must be quite a comical bloke.
He certainly had *me* in stitches:
I got all the points of his joke.

The moral must be that all humor
Depends upon your point of view.
It's comic to be all in stitches:
Except when the joke is on you!

# Practice

There's one little quirk of the language
Which gives the mere patient a fright.
They say this is where they're "in practice."
Best wait 'til they've got it just right!

# Symbiosis

These doctors are very supportive
Of all of their colleagues' careers.
In one of the hospital buildings
They're cutting up noses and ears –

While just down the hall are their fellows
(The sheet metal crew of the mix).
You pay the first experts to maim things
You then pay the others to fix.

*Fire poppy; its association with fire
and pain-killers make this an appropriate flower
to link surgery and radiation.*

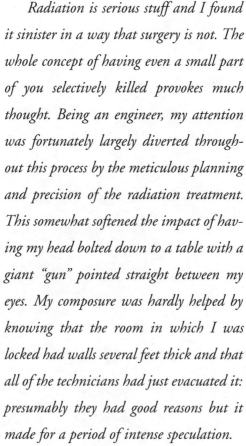

*Radiation is serious stuff and I found it sinister in a way that surgery is not. The whole concept of having even a small part of you selectively killed provokes much thought. Being an engineer, my attention was fortunately largely diverted throughout this process by the meticulous planning and precision of the radiation treatment. This somewhat softened the impact of having my head bolted down to a table with a giant "gun" pointed straight between my eyes. My composure was hardly helped by knowing that the room in which I was locked had walls several feet thick and that all of the technicians had just evacuated it: presumably they had good reasons but it made for a period of intense speculation.*

# *Radiation I*

Bombardment with electrons creates havoc with the cells
That make up melanoma, or so the doctor tells.
This talent for destruction may well end cancer's days.
But what about the healthy bits that also catch the rays?

The cheeks and gums and nose and skin all end up very sore.
The tumor may be toast, but all the rest feels truly raw.
No doubt it's worth the anguish in the search for longer days.
But there's one special problem which is sore in other ways:

My face was long distinguished (camouflaged's a better word)
By yards and yards of whiskers, all by razor undisturbed.
Then radiation struck and, on my right side's face and chin,
Laid down a random pattern made of shiny, smooth bare skin.

So now I have to shave those scattered patches that still sprout,
An extra daily ritual I could well get by without.
If doctors have the wherewithal to kill each cancer cell,
How come they couldn't bother to take *all* my beard as well?

# *Radiation II*

The principal that lies behind the use of radiations,
Is really rather eerie if you choose to think it through.
You're cooked inside a microwave for varying durations,
Deliberately damaging the suspect parts of you.

Each individual treatment is designed to cause attrition,
But only to the tissues in the area of concern.
The hope is that the healthy bits will brave this repetition
And never quite be broiled beyond the point of no return.

The cancer, though, for all its nasty habit of aggression,
Possesses subtle weakness in its powers of repair.
So if you toast it often it may fall into depression
And end up shrinking harmlessly, a loss you'll gladly bear.

Control of such a process is a major undertaking.
This fine, selective killing must be judged exactly right.
Some very nasty damage can be caused by over-baking
And tumors quickly tell you if the treatment was too light.

In my case I was lucky, for they cooked me to perfection.
Although my face was painful I could stand that any day.
So far as can be told from all their gadgets of detection,
When things got really hot the cancer upped and went away!

*Another cactus. With its mixture of*
*spine and flower it is well suited to the pain and promise*
*of radiation therapy.*

*Any degree of disfigurement is a frightening prospect, particularly when its degree is unknown and you have been spending time in hospital corridors seeing the afflictions of so many others. In contrast to their problems, a bent nose is a minor matter indeed and the loss of a beard a positive blessing.*

# *My Nose*

I'm used to the staring in India
For there I looked quite out of place.
But now that it's happening in England
I think it's to do with my face.

I once had a nose that was normal,
Not roman, retroussé or hooked.
Now half of it's gone in the bucket,
Just leaving, the last time I looked,

A mixture of styles most unusual.
The left is still much as before,
But now, when I look out the window,
My right nostril points at the door.

Still, this is a time to be thankful
For having a nose there to show.
Who cares if it's perfect or crooked?
At least I have something to blow!

# *Bare-Faced Robbery*

This desmoplastic robber broke and entered in my face.
In guise non-melanotic stayed and burglarized the place.
What did he steal, what took he as he roamed beneath my skin?
We cannot yet be certain that the final toll is in.

My natural appearance quickly vanished in his haul,
My nose and cheek disfigured by the surgeon's wrecking ball.
Topped off by radiation's random stripping of my beard,
Though all has healed completely, the result looks kind of weird!

These, though, are not the outcomes that will have the most import,
No scar can have the impact of a total change of thought.
The uninvited felon who so rudely marred my face
Has left behind a legacy which time cannot erase.

He stole the immortality that most of us assume,
And go right on believing until laid into our tomb.
But in its place he left behind a gift of priceless worth.
A germ of understanding, unexpected second birth.

We're not on earth to pass the time or simply take up space;
We're here to use our talents to reflect God's loving grace.
It's quality, not quantity that forms the mark we make.
That robber surely left a gift more precious than his "take".

# *On Losing a Close Friend*

Farewell to you, companion of my life
Who, from the first, was closer than my wife;
Stayed by my side through happiness and trouble,
Right from the time you were a little stubble.

For twenty years I wore you like a mask,
Inseparable, however cruel the task.
Sunshine and snow alike you loved to brave,
Your only fear was of a real close shave.

For all that time we traveled cheek to cheek.
Cut off from you the future would look bleak.
Will you be missed? Why yes, for to deny
That we were close would be a barefaced lie.

Now you've succumbed to radiation's blast,
Merely a shadow of your bushy past.
Though it may feel, and look, a little weird
I'll just make do with life without a beard.

# *Partly Confused*

When small children draw a face,
Each bit has its proper place.
Eyes up there and mouth below –
Not much doubt where those parts go.

Even tinies, I suppose,
Know just where to place the nose.
And the smallest little dears
Easily locate the ears.

Why then after all this time,
When I've nearly reached my prime,
When my face I've oft perused,
Do I get these bits confused?

Stuck right in the middle here
Is just about one half an ear.
How that surgeon must have laughed,
When he chose that ear to graft.

It's the right one that he chose
As spare parts to fix the nose.
Now, as well as sniff and smell,
This same nose can hear as well.

When I have a cold it's funny
Having half an ear that's runny.
It would be politer if
I'd blow my ear and stop the sniff.

Supercilious aristos
Look at people down their nose.
While for me to wear a sneer –
I'd be looking down my ear.

Very few throughout the globe
Have a nose that sports a lobe.
Or, and these are proven facts,
No-one's nose gets blocked with wax.

As for me, I just don't care,
Ears are neither here or there.
Of the parts that disappeared,
I'd prefer to find my beard!

*Cancer's most sinister property is probably its ability to pop up in new parts of the body, to 'metastasize' as our learned medical friends say. This makes it impossible to declare a conclusive victory over a skin cancer just because the skin itself is clear. Understanding the status of the disease is thus very difficult for the patient, and indeed for the doctors. Even when the news is good, there is always a feeling that claiming victory comes very close to issuing an invitation to a new lump to appear, probably somewhere unexpected and, to say the least, inconvenient. Check x-rays or scans become a routine facet of life, with the order forms simply and chillingly marked "mets" — short for the dreaded metastases.*

# *Metastasis*

It's gone, it's out, it's done at last,
The surface of my face has passed
Their microscopic scrutiny,
And offers further life to me.

The wound is closed, the graft is done,
A brand new lease on life is won.
And, for a while, each caring voice
Can find a reason to rejoice.

Yet hid beneath this happy theme
A darker truth can just be seen.
Metastasis, that evil word,
Though only whispered, can be heard.

The tumor was too deep, too wide,
To hope to keep its cells inside.
No doubt a few have wandered free
In search of a new destiny.

How fare my warriors in their fights
Against those dark melanocytes?
Where do they lurk, these quisling cells?
So far no pain or swelling tells.

An eerie feeling this, I've found,
Being both prize and battleground.
Waiting to hear how well we stayed
Their latest, silent, deadly raid.

# *Clear Scans*

Clear scans!
Words of great promise,
What is their meaning for me?
Clear scans!  Can it be really true
Nothing is left there to see?

Clear scans!
Dare I rejoice in them
Taunting the gods with my health?
Clear scans!   Maybe they're teasing me,
Waiting their moment with stealth.

Clear scans!
Nothing has changed for you,
Ask not how long you will live.
Clear scans!  Use every minute well.
Take all the present can give.

*Lily of the Valley,*
*celebrating the 'return of joy'*

*My new-found appreciation of the joys of everyday life was probably never more acute than during an April walk round the village of Blockley in the picturesque English Cotswolds district. I cannot imagine anyone who has experienced that beauty, tranquility and sense of rightness across the centuries, not feeling healed and challenged to find small doses of the same medicine somewhere in his ordinary world.*

# *Alternative Medicine*

I have been taking medicine for my heart
these last few days,
A remedy available to all, free of all cost,
devoid of side effects.

One dose, when taken daily, clears the brain,
puts stress into its place;
Adds vigor to the step and peace to sleep;
sends cancer in retreat.

The name of the new wonder-dealing drug
that offers hopes like these?
It is an ancient annual gift of God, called
Cotswolds in Spring.

There are a hundred herbs within this brew,
each magic in its way.
The butter cream of stone, mellowed with age,
narcissus' golden glow.

Free rivers singing in the sun, a tiny garden's wealth.
Sweeping green hills, dotted white with sheep,
The ancient tower with flying vanes,
the sacred yard beneath.

Drink you this medicine quietly, with respect,
for this is heaven's shadow,
Placed here to calm and heal men's souls
and bring their bodies peace.

*It's not wholly unreasonable or morbid to think occasionally of death when under-going treatment for cancer. In fact, it's a very good idea when it leads to sensible practical planning and arrangements, a degree of acceptance of what might come next or, more happily, an enhanced appre-ciation of and joy in life. The next verses reflect some of my thoughts as the reality of my mortality sank in, maybe for the first time in my life.*

# *Life Expectancy*

The length of life expectancy
Is suddenly of great import.
There's real curiosity
To know if it be long or short.

The doctor says, in kind attempt
To set aside our fears,
"There's really quite a fighting chance
You'll last for five more years.

Some two in three or three in four
Can stretch it out that long.
Of course, it could be more or less;
Statistics can be wrong."

This wasn't altogether quite
The span we'd had in view.
But it was far too early
To determine what is true.

The time to ask such questions
Is when they've cause to know
If my pet melanoma's
Simply gone - or gone 'below.'

One bonus from this cancer
Is an understanding how,
By counting on the future,
We can steal the joy from now.

We made no reservation
At the moment of our birth,
No Visa confirmation
Of a certain stay on earth.

Until our time we'll simply
Take our blessings as they are,
Be grateful for each sunrise
Every flower, bird and star.

# *The Burning Fuse*

This much we know, all we who now draw breath
Must face the final certainty of death.
That theory's fine, accepted, filed away
For action on some yet far distant day.

One word, though, is enough to change this dream,
Shatter assumptions that have reigned supreme.
One tiny hint of cancer changes all,
Sweeps all the clouds from round the crystal ball.

Cancer's no theory, generality,
This dose of truth is personal to me.
My fuse is lit, burns now towards its close,
I see its flame: its length, though, no-one knows.

Time's quantity is fixed, though still unknown.
The quality's a matter all our own.
We only can determine how we spend
The time remaining to the fuse's end.

A new test this for our philosophy,
To navigate this sure uncertainty.
To live and love with honor, joy and grace
While such a fuse is sparking in our face.

Its smoke obscures our vision of the way
But, once we learn to focus on today,
Ignoring any future, short or long,
Just for today we can be kind and strong.

This cancer then has proved to be a boon;
This knowledge that it all could end quite soon
Has blown away our sense of endless sway;
And in its place has given us, today.

Today's one day on which we can depend
Whatever joys or knocks the future send.
Today's our first best chance to heed the call
To live for others if we live at all.

Thus wisdom of the ancients is made new
For us, a blessing given but to few.
Now immortality is in the past
We're free to live each day as if our last.

# Reminders

Most of us at work or play,
Make the same unsaid assumption
That we'll live for many a day.
Probably a real presumption.

So we need a better teacher
Who'll remind us every day:
Of the truth we need to guide us
Through this transient earthly stay.

Melanoma's been my teacher,
Leaving, plain for me to see,
Marks I cannot but acknowledge
As the tracks of destiny.

Each time I see my reflection,
Notice that my nose is weird,
Or whenever I am shaving
My bedraggled, patchy beard,

I'm reminded, willy-nilly,
Of my fragile mortal state.
What a blunt but blessed reminder
That each day could be The Date.

# The Cancer Game

Cancer is a silly contest,
One you wouldn't play for fun.
There are many ways of losing
But no way to know you've won.

Winning's really losing later,
Fending off the beast's return.
Not a final, clear departure
Leaving tumors far astern.

Well, so what? The sun is shining,
Scans are clear and hopes can soar.
This fine day we're surely winning.
None could really ask for more.

# Part 3:

# *Afterthoughts*

*Campanula 'harebell',*
*traditionally standing for gratitude*

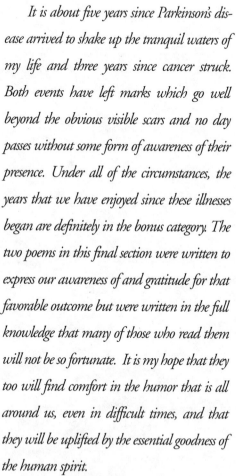

It is about five years since Parkinson's disease arrived to shake up the tranquil waters of my life and three years since cancer struck. Both events have left marks which go well beyond the obvious visible scars and no day passes without some form of awareness of their presence. Under all of the circumstances, the years that we have enjoyed since these illnesses began are definitely in the bonus category. The two poems in this final section were written to express our awareness of and gratitude for that favorable outcome but were written in the full knowledge that many of those who read them will not be so fortunate. It is my hope that they too will find comfort in the humor that is all around us, even in difficult times, and that they will be uplifted by the essential goodness of the human spirit.

# *Thanks*

To you, dear friends, who showed your care
By phone or letter, thought or prayer,
These lines at last will bring some word
Of what's transpired since last you heard.

Four months have passed since those dark days
When I soaked up the healing rays.
Now is the time to count the score
And find out if we're in for more.

The news? As good as it could be.
No trace of cancer could they see.
It may still lurk in some dark cells,
But – just for now – Ring Out the Bells!

The doctors were beyond compare,
Blending their skill with human care.
But, just as vital as their arts,
Has been support from loving hearts.

This battle's won, but not the war
So please keep caring as before.
Your calls and letters, laughs and hugs
Are proving most addictive drugs!

# *In Summary*

Ignore the scars, forget the rays,
Today I'm rich in countless ways.
I woke beside a loving wife,
Another day of blessed life.

The sky was clear, the clouds were gone,
And here and there a star still shone.
The night sky glistened overhead
The east horizon rimmed with red.

The mountains show themselves in gray,
Sharpening as they sense the day.
Gray turns to purple then to pinks
As night's last cap of darkness shrinks.

A golden halo grows about
The point from which will soon break out
The sun, whose blazing, blinding light
Asserts its power to conquer night.

All these delights, ah! here's the rub,
I see from my Jacuzzi tub!
Warm water surges from the jets,
About as good as living gets.

Is cancer dead? Well...not for sure,
It may still have a dread encore.
But there's no tumor can erase
The joy I harvest from such days.

And Parkinson, is he still here,
To shake my hand and spill my beer?
Of course, and will be to the end.
We simply treat him as a friend.

While breaking dawns are there to view
And nature's pageant's out there too,
My fortune grows with every breath.
With such great wealth, what fear in death?

# Part 4:
# *Photograph Album*

*Most of the photographs are either the property of the author or have been extracted from his medical records through the cooperation of the doctors and their staffs. Other photographs were provided by the doctors themselves and the University of Washington Medical Center and are gratefully acknowledged.*

*The "house up on the hill"*

page 14

*"Dr. Hutton,
who doesn't miss
nuttin'…"*
page 53

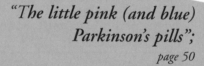

*"The little pink (and blue)
Parkinson's pills";*
page 50

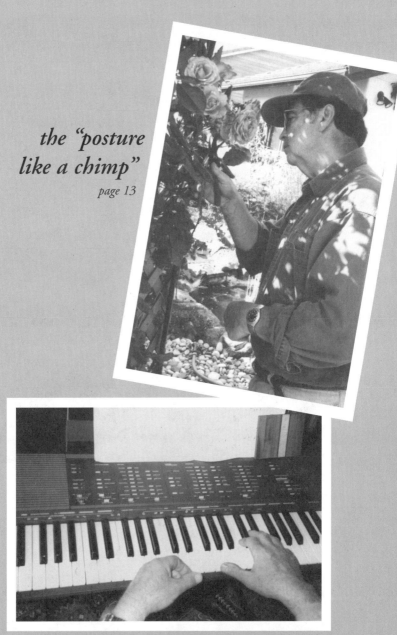

the "posture
like a chimp"
page 13

"turning my Mozart to defeat"
page 25

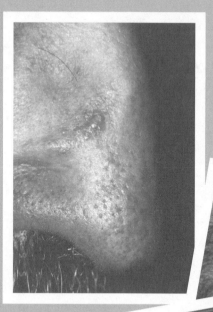

*"mighty oaks from little acorns grow"*
page 61

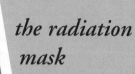

*the radiation mask*
page 78

*"At least I have something to blow."* page 83

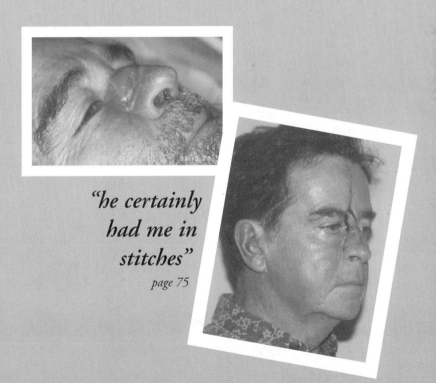

*"he certainly had me in stitches"* page 75

# "The doctors were beyond compare"
page 103

Paul Thompson ... "the derm..."

Craig Murakami
... the surgeon

Mary Austen-Seymour ...
the radiation oncologist

The University of Washington Medical Center

# *Acknowledgements*

Many people made significant contributions towards the creation of this book and we are grateful to them all.

The fundamental role was of course played by the medical personnel who created the most essential basis for the book by keeping me not only alive but cheerful and reasonably functional for the past five years. This group includes, for example, the nurses who changed dressings in the middle of the night as well as the doctors who played such skilled roles; receptionists as well as dentists, insurance agents and hospital accountants. The way they all do their work can make a big difference and they provided a great boost to both of us.

Before I can write poetry, I need to feel some purpose in life and that need has been amply provided throughout these years by family and friends. Our children flew across the world to be with us at times when their warmth and wisdom could be really helpful; friends from around the globe sent their messages of caring and support and many continue to do so after several years. It would be very ungrateful not to be cheerful under these circumstances.

It is a long way from writing occasional lines to celebrate a family occasion, to publishing a book such as this. Much of the courage required for such a step has come from our friends, some of whom have been very insistent on the subject for years. It would never have happened without their confidence and we are grateful. We have also been greatly helped with the mechanics of book production by the staff at Elton Wolf Publishing who made critical contributions to the final form of the book.

## *Anthony and Iris Edey*

Anthony and Iris Edey were both born in England and met in church in London in 1955. They were married in 1959, lived in Central Africa for the next 15 years and, since coming to the USA in 1974, have lived in such diverse states as Washington, Colorado and Georgia before making their home on a beach in the Pacific Northwest. Their two children and six grandchildren have all chosen to live in England.

Anthony is a mining engineer who worked in the Zambian copper mining industry before joining a consulting company in the US and, from 1983, working for a company which he formed with Iris to support their diverse careers. This venture kept him totally busy until 1995 when ill-health struck, as recounted in this book. His many interests, after family, include music, gardening, bread-making and the English language. While he has always written "silly verse" for family occasions

and student reviews, and has produced or edited a large tonnage of technical material, this is his first venture into print.

Iris showed her artistic talent at an early age but could not develop it seriously until the 1980's when she was able to put her interim careers (as couturier dressmaker, sales assistant in London's fashionable West End, nanny, wife and mother) behind her. After much experimenting with media and subjects, she is now totally focused on flowers, drawing them and painting them from life in the most demanding medium — transparent watercolor. Her work has been in great demand wherever it has been displayed or her travels have taken her. It has to compete, though, with her equal passions for gardening, travel, yoga and small children.

Copies of this book can be ordered from

Iris Enterprises, Inc.

32 West Seashore Lane

Sequim, WA 98382

or

Call: 360.683.4721

Fax: 360.683.2977

or Email:

irisbooks@hotmail.com

edeysqm@olypen.com